Now hear this, ANDY CAPP

Reginald Smythe

FAWCETT GOLD MEDAL • NEW YORK

A Fawcett Gold Medal Book
Published by Ballantine Books
Copyright © 1982 by Mirror Group Newspapers Ltd. and
Syndication International Ltd.
Distributed by North America Syndicate, Inc., a subsidiary of The Hearst
Corporation.

Library of Congress Catalog Card Number: 87-91010

ISBN 0-449-13204-8

Manufactured in the United States of America

First Edition: February 1988

9-29 — Smythe

7-31

8-2

ANDY LOOKS SHATTERED THIS MORNIN', FLO

HE WAS AT HIS REGIMENTAL REUNION LAST NIGHT — REAL HEAVY WORK

HEAVY WORK?

8-5

YEAH, YOU KNOW — DIGGIN' UP THE PAST

8-14

8-31

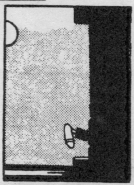

9-6

9-8

WHERE'S 'E STAYIN', FLO?

WHERE IT'S CHEAP, RUBE — WITH 'IS MOTHER

'OPE YOU DON'T MIND, FLO, BUT I'VE TALKED MY SON INTO COMIN' BACK TO YOU

AS LONG AS YOU TELL 'IM TO MAKE IT *NEXT* WEEK

I MUST SAY, FLO, YOU TOOK THAT VERY CALMLY

THE WAY TO TAKE THINGS AS THEY COME, RUBE, IS TO STAGGER THE UNPLEASANT THINGS FAR ENOUGH APART

9-18

NOW'S YOUR CHANCE, MATE ..... JUST LOOK AT THE STATE 'E'S IN —

TAKE YOU ON AT DARTS FOR A FIVER, ANDY?

SORRY, PERCY — SOME OTHER TIME, EH?

9-22

I WAS FORGETTIN' — 'E'S ALWAYS SOBER ENOUGH TO KNOW WHEN 'E'S DRUNK

IS CHALKIE IN A BETTER MOOD, RUBE?

9-25

NO, FLO. 'E GETS SO BORED, DOESN'T KNOW WHAT TO DO WITH 'IMSELF

NOT LIKE ME, EH, PET? I'M *NEVER* SHORT OF THINGS TO DO

THAT'S TRUE. TROUBLE IS, 'E ALWAYS DOES WHAT 'E *CAN* DO INSTEAD OF THE SCORES OF THINGS 'E *SHOULD* DO

MEN

I SHOULD 'AVE BEEN CLOSED HOURS AGO! C'MON NOW, GET Y'SELF 'OME — *PLEASE*

'E'S A DEVIL TO GET RID OF

LET'S SEE NOW — FRONT DOOR BOLTED, BACK DOOR BOLTED, WINDOWS LOCKED

SAFE AT LAST

9-27

....I DON'T KNOW, THOUGH. A COUPLE OF WEEKS AGO 'E CAME DOWN THE CHIMNEY

9-28

'OW DID YOU GET ON, PET?

I SHOULD GET THE JOB—I WALTZED THROUGH THE ENTRANCE EXAM

9-29

WHAT D'YOU THINK, RUBE?

SAME AS YOU, FLO. WHEN 'E KNOWS ALL THE ANSWERS 'E MOST LIKELY MISUNDERSTOOD THE QUESTIONS

IT'S OPENIN' TIME, ANDY—!

I'M RATHER BUSY, CHALKIE — I'M PLOTTIN' OUT OUR FINANCIAL COURSE!

BILL BILL FINAL DEMAND BILL

THAT'S OKAY, PET — I'LL TAKE OVER

10-1

IF 'E'D LEAVE THINGS TO CHANCE, THEY'D BE BETTER

10-2

I CAN BE VERY NICE TO A BLOKE IF 'E TREATS ME RIGHT....

TOP UP THE LITTLE DARLIN'S GLASS, JACKIE

10-4

WOULD YOU BE NICE ENOUGH TO EXCUSE ME FOR A GAME OF DARTS WI' THE LADS?

THIS BLOKE EXPECTS TOO *LITTLE* OF A GIRL

10-5

10-6

10-9

OOH! MY POOR NECK AN' BACK! I FEEL ABOUT EIGHTY - THANKS TO YOU!

AN' I FEEL NINETY - THANKS TO YOU! THESE DAYS YOU NEVER QUESTION ME ABOUT WHICH BARMAID I'VE BEEN CHASIN' AFTER!!

10-15

THERE'S ALWAYS SOMEONE WORSE OFF THAN YOURSELF, EH?

WOULD YOU KEEP AN EYE ON THE HOUSE, RUBE? ANDY'S TAKIN' ME AWAY FOR A COUPLE O' DAYS!

'COURSE, I WILL

10-18

I'M REALLY LOOKIN' FORWARD TO IT, SWEET'EART - IT'LL BE A LOVELY CHANGE

LET'S SEE NOW. TWO CLEAN SHIRTS, DARTS, SNOOKER CUE, CARDS. THAT'S *ME* PACKED, PET

RUBE-

YES?

FORGET IT!!

10-20

I HOPE THEY MAKE A GO OF IT. SO MANY MARRIAGES END UP ON THE ROCKS THESE DAYS

JUST MARRIED

MIND YOU, THERE ARE THE HEARTENING ONES — THE CAPPS, FOR INSTANCE, NEVER BEEN SEPARATED...

APART FROM THE OCCASIONAL TIME BY THE POLICE

10-21

THIS CAN'T GO ON. STANDIN' IN THE SAME OLD SPOT AN' GIVIN' THE SAME OLD LECTURE. YOU MUST BE AS SICK OF IT AS I AM

YOU'RE RIGHT, SWEET'EART.....

'OW ABOUT DOIN' IT FROM THE TOP O' THE STAIRS?

10-22

10-23

10-26

STOP STARIN'

I WAS JUST WONDERIN' ABOUT THAT LASS OVER THERE —

10-27

I THINK SHE MIGHT BE A MODEL—

SHE WEARS 'ER CLOTHES WELL...

I WEAR *MINE* WELL, TOO! I'VE WORN THIS COAT FOR FOUR YEARS, AND AS FOR THESE SHOES—!

OH, LOR, 'ERE WE GO AGAIN

WINK

10-29

SEE THAT, PET — TAKES YOU BACK, EH?

SURE DOES

I PRACTICALLY THREW MYSELF AT *HIM*, TOO — I MEANT TO THROW MYSELF AT HIS MATE, BUT I'D HAD A FEW

11-1

11-3

11-6

I DID IT AGAIN, FLO! SCORED THE WINNIN' GOAL FROM A PENALTY IN THE VERY LAST MINUTE

11-18

NO DOUBT ABOUT IT— SOMEBODY UP THERE LIKES ME

I'M NOT SO SURE ABOUT SOME OF US DOWN 'ERE, MATE!

I CAN'T BELIEVE IT, RUBE! FIRST I WIN THE SWEEPSTAKE IN THE CANTEEN AN' THEN I GET A FULL-HOUSE!

PITY YOU'VE GOT TO TELL ANDY

OH, I'LL 'AVE TO, RUBE

'ELLO, PET. BOY, WHAT A DAY I'VE 'AD—

LOOK, DON'T TELL ME ABOUT *YOUR* DAY, AN' I WON'T TELL YOU ABOUT *MINE*

12-3

YOU'RE A A WITNESS —I DID *TRY* TO TELL 'IM

12-4

12-13

12-16

COR! WHAT A DAY I'VE HAD, RUBE —

12-20

YOU KNOW THAT CLAPPED OUT SEWIN' MACHINE OF MINE? I MANAGED TO SELL IT FOR A TENNER...

OH, LOVELY

AN' REMEMBER THE THREE POUNDS I LENT TO ADA ALL THAT TIME AGO? SHE PAID ME BACK TODAY...

LOVELY

AN' THEN WHEN I GOT 'OME THIS EVENIN' I FOUND ANDY 'AD PACKED 'IS BAGS AN' GONE OFF AGAIN

'OW LUCKY CAN YOU GET?!

BINGO

12-22